# My Wish For Tomorrow

## WORDS AND PICTURES FROM CHILDREN AROUND THE WORLD

A collaboration between Jim Henson
Publishing and the United Nations

FOREWORD BY *Nelson R. Mandela,*
*President of the Republic of South Africa*

INTRODUCTION BY *Boutros Boutros-Ghali,*
*Secretary-General of the United Nations*

TAMBOURINE BOOKS  NEW YORK

Printed in the United States of America. The text type is 16 pt. Bodoni.

ISBN 0-688-14451-1 (trade)
ISBN 0-688-14456-X (lib. bdg.)
Cataloging in Publication data is available.

3   5   7   9   10   8   6   4   2
First edition

## FOREWORD

Over thirty years ago I declared that I cherished the ideal of a democratic and free society in which all persons could live together in harmony and with equal opportunities.

This dream, based on respect for the fundamental rights of all persons, is what the United Nations stands for. In South Africa it is a dream that is coming true.

In reading this book one will notice that children from around the world express these same hopes. This is a very encouraging sign, and theirs is a voice that deserves to be heard.

The fiftieth anniversary of the United Nations and the sentiments expressed in this book are a celebration of the growing realization of that dream. On behalf of the people of South Africa—and especially on behalf of our children—I commend this book to all the children throughout the world.

*Nelson R. Mandela*
*President of the Republic of South Africa*

## INTRODUCTION

Ever since its inception in 1945, the United Nations has been working to make this world a better place for our children—to ensure peace, justice, and prosperity for our future generations.

With this book, created in celebration of the fiftieth anniversary of the United Nations, we can hear the voices of children from around the world expressing their wishes, hopes, and dreams for a better future. We must listen to them, for their words—and their drawings—carry fundamental truths. And, in the freshness and simplicity of their vision, the children can help focus our hearts, our minds, and our efforts on what is truly important.

*Boutros Boutros-Ghali*
*Secretary-General of the United Nations*

A new world
A blue world
A sea world
A green world
A happy world
A laughing world
It's getting too late.

–Lauren Kimberly Pye, Age 8, United States

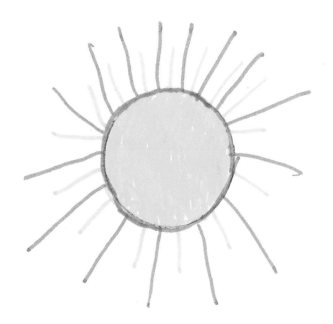

I would like to educate the people
to share the world with animals and
trees so they will not kill them. Everybody
has its place: the animals, the trees, and us.

–Kristel Acevedo Nevermann, Age 6, Costa Rica

I wish I could ask the fairies to make all trees grow
sweets for children.

–Adrian Moss, Age 6, Malawi

If a wall falls down cranes can build it up again; but
if a friendship wall falls, it's you that has to do the building.
Stop fighting and be friends.

–Meadhbh Long, Age 9, Ireland

I wish that there would be no disadvantaged people, and that everybody could see, hear, laugh, speak, run, love, play. . . . If there were no disabilities that would be my wish.

–David Gray, Age 12, Australia

I would wish for the ozone hole to close. I wish AIDS would be cured and that children without parents can have new parents to look after them.

–Kevin Mclean, Age 11, Malawi

I wish I could behave better in my world.

–Navin Naunam Miangales, Age 11, Trinidad

I wish all adults would have a good heart that
they will always understand the children.

–Cynthia Barreda Vilchez, Age 9, Peru

Wish: That young people wouldn't forget
old people.

–Renato Reyes, Age 4, Peru

I wish the most civilized nations could express their knowledge to other nations.

–Wambua Kyalo, Age 9, Kenya

I wish that every bomb, every shot, every death would be replaced by the smile of a child.

–Daniela Eduarda de Magalhaes Carneiro, Age 11, Portugal

I wish that I was the president, and I would make sure that every poor person was rich.

–Maggie Nash McCaffrey, Age 6, United States

## PEACE IN THE WORLD

All I want is a little peace please.
All I want is peace.
War in the world is everywhere.
All I want is peace.
I want peace in the North,
Peace in the South,
Peace in the East and West.
All I want is peace.
Peace in the hearts of all the leaders
in different nations of the world.
Peace is so great.
Thank you peace.

–Nadezsha Elizabeth Ann Perreira, Age 10, Guyana

In my new world all must speak little, but speak the truth.

–Vijay Vardhan, Age unknown, India

I wish everyone would love each other for what they are and that nobody would have to put on an act to be liked.

—Akanksha Hazari, Age 11 1/2, China

Wish: If people did not have far to go that they would use horse carriages instead of cars. P.S. That is good for the environment.

—Marielouise Bech Madsen, Age 10, Denmark

We wish everyone could be kind to other people. We believe if one is kind to others, wars might be disappeared in the world.

—Songyee Lee and Aram Lee (twins), Age 11, South Korea

My wish is to make a big flying carpet so that I can fly on it
around the world to make friends.

–Sonali Handalage, Age 8, Sri Lanka

I wish everyone would be friends—nobody was ever sad
and nobody ever felt left out in games and in the spring
and summer months many fields were filled with sweet
smelling flowers and the world was alright and safe.
That's how I wish the world to be.

–Rachel Tsang, Age 9, China

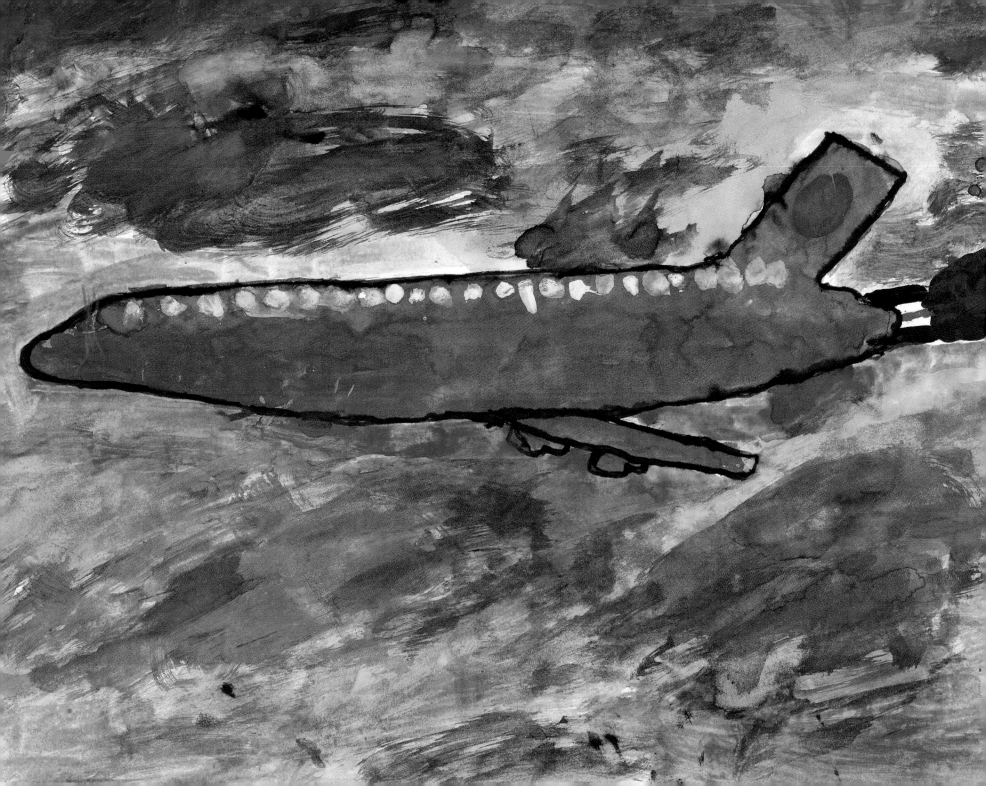

I wish that the parents who have children would not throw them away.

–Allison Mary Lobb, Age 10, Zimbabwe

If I was granted one wish to make the world a better place, I would wish that people should live without fear.

–Danwathie Devi Persaud, Age 11, Guyana

I wish that people would stop violences and share even if it is just a crumb.

–Chellis Williams, Age 8, Jamaica

I would like to see people carpool with each other.

–Ja-Ling Sethavanish, Age 10, Thailand


Let everybody be smiling and happy.

–Marlene Fontbonne, Age 11, France


I would like all cities to be designed for disabled people.

–Agnieszka Fiedler, Age 12, Poland

I wish that from the sounds of a violin came beautiful music, that would be heard all over the world and that all the hearts would be filled with love.

–Lucas E. De Abreu, Age 10, Brazil

I wish that it would snow.

–Michael Bernd Nolting, Age 9, Namibia

I wish people had clothes to wear.

–Laura Marvin, Age 7 1/2, England


If the stomach is filled up it is easier to keep peace.

–Ida Sjursø, Age 11, Norway


We have to build a better world loving each other,
selfishness shouldn't exist, race differences, social
differences, and repression shouldn't exist.

–Fanny Perez Quezada, Age 9, Ecuador

I wish I was a butterfly
So I would fly so high in the sky
I would spread pollen all around
And let flowers bloom happily all around.
What I wouldn't like is for someone to catch me
For then I wouldn't have my liberty.

–Vaani Rambhojun, Age 8, Mauritius

I want the world to be a good place. . . .
I want the sugar, flour to become cheap.

–Mumbua Mackenzi, Age 12, Kenya

I wish people could keep their
promises that they make for peace.

–Cathy Fisher, Age 10, South Africa

Wish: UN must make more space agencies to know the
universe better (it is necessary if we abandon this one.)

–S. Özüm Basta, Age 11, Turkey

Peace is the best of my wishes. I would adore to see one
day, everyone (all over the world) give a hug and say,
How are you?

–Catia Sofia Feiléiro Lopes, Age 9, Portugal

No pollution. No murder. No diseases. No drugs. Maybe that's too many wishes—just one better world please.

–Diva Arun-Datwani, Age 6, Japan

A clean world.
A world with peace.
A fun world.
A better world.
A big world.
That everyone can be free.
That all this shall become true.

–Eduardo Blanco, Age 11, Argentina

I wish that people did not make fun of other people.

–Stephanie Sotiris, Age 7, England

I wish for my friend to get better, for the weather to be good, to have clean water, and for everybody to be well.

–Pandora Bilali, Age 6, Greece

I wish there was clothes for us all as it's cold now and some children are naked.

–Lyomba Stella, Age 10, Namibia

I wish that elephants may be kept safe from hunters otherwise there will be no more left like the dodoes.

–Allison Maxillan, Age 10, Malawi

**To have peace and health and trees for oxygen.**

–Vicky Theodorou, Age 7, Greece

**Do not trash the forest.**

–Bryce Alexander Marshall, Age 6, Australia

From today on, even a crumb of bread mustn't be thrown away. . . . As long as a single child is hungry we must sympathize with him. Let's say no to starvation.

–Maria Del Mar Casas, Age 11, Spain

My wish is house.

–Fortunate Miambo, Age 7, Zimbabwe

My wish is happy families.

–Everest Waeni, Age 9, Zimbabwe

I wish people wouldn't sleep in the streets and everyone would have a house, no matter how small.

–Gyve Safavi, Age 10, Iran

My wish is to see more happy children around me with more food and water on their tables.

–Noura Basim Haddad, Age 8, Jordan

I wish the world becomes safer for everyone and people don't have to worry about keeping their doors unlocked or even letting their children walk to school by themselves.

–Rebecca Ann Story, Age 12, Australia

Mayra/94
Gquil - Ecuador

**I wish the world would be happy forever after.**

–Dumolone Dube, Age 6, Zimbabwe

If you were granted one wish to make the world a better place, what would it be? To help celebrate the fiftieth birthday of the United Nations in 1995, the UN and Jim Henson Productions asked children from every part of the world that question. The book you have just read contains a small selection of their answers and their drawings.

Following are just a few of the members of the United Nations family working hard to make this a better world.

**UNITED NATIONS CHILDREN'S FUND (UNICEF)**
Helps children all over the world to live happy and healthy lives.

**UNITED NATIONS HIGH COMMISSIONER FOR REFUGEES (UNHCR)**
Protects people who have had to flee their homes because of natural disasters, fighting, or fear that they might be harmed because of their race, religion, or politics.

**UNITED NATIONS ENVIRONMENT PROGRAMME (UNEP)**
Works to fight the spread of deserts and the destruction of forests, to clean up our seas, and to protect endangered species and ecosystems.

**UNITED NATIONS CENTRE FOR HUMAN SETTLEMENTS (HABITAT)**
Helps countries provide housing and other services, especially for poor people living in cities.

**UNITED NATIONS DEVELOPMENT PROGRAM (UNDP)**
Helps countries develop their natural and human resources.

**UNITED NATIONS INTERNATIONAL DRUG CONTROL PROGRAMME (UNDCP)**
Works to stop the spread of illegal drugs around the world.

**UNITED NATIONS POPULATION FUND (UNFPA)**
Helps countries manage growing populations.

**WORLD HEALTH ORGANIZATION (WHO)**
Works to keep all the people of the world healthy.

**FOOD AND AGRICULTURE ORGANIZATION (FAO)**
Helps people have enough to eat by teaching them how to improve their farms, forests, and fisheries.

**UNITED NATIONS EDUCATIONAL, SCIENTIFIC, AND CULTURAL ORGANIZATION (UNESCO)**
Helps countries cooperate, using education, science, culture, and communication to make the world a safer and more peaceful place.

**WORLD INTELLECTUAL PROPERTY ORGANIZATION (WIPO)**
Protects the rights of inventors, authors, artists, composers, and musicians.

**WORLD METEOROLOGICAL ORGANIZATION (WMO)**
Gives accurate information about the weather, climate, and environment to people around the world.

**INTERNATIONAL TELECOMMUNICATION UNION (ITU)**
Improves telephone, radio, and television service around the world by assigning radio frequencies and satellite locations.

**UNIVERSAL POSTAL UNION (UPU)**
Makes the rules that help mail travel from country to country.

**INTERNATIONAL CIVIL AVIATION ORGANIZATION (ICAO)**
Sets rules for air traffic and helps make sure that people all over the world can fly safely.

**INTERNATIONAL ATOMIC ENERGY AGENCY (IAEA)**
Helps nations safely develop and use atomic energy for peaceful purposes.

**INTERNATIONAL LABOUR ORGANIZATION (ILO)**
Tries to make sure that working people everywhere are treated fairly.

For more information about the United Nations and its agencies, contact the Public Inquiries Unit, United Nations Headquarters, New York, NY 10017
Telephone: (212) 963-4475

# ACKNOWLEDGMENTS

Every effort has been made to properly identify the name, age, and country of every child who has contributed wishes and artwork for this book. Any errors or omissions are inadvertent, and the publisher will be pleased to make the necessary corrections in future printings.

Special thanks to the hundreds of artists who have donated work for this book. The following children's work has been included:

NATALIA FERNÁNDEZ MENDOZA, Age 10, Chile, title page
ROBERTO CARLOS MORAGA VÁSQUEZ, Age 7, Chile, page 6
SAMANTHA LOUISE EDDIE, Age 11, Australia, pages 7, 12, and 16
CONSTANZA DEL PILAR MORALES GALLARDO, Age 9, Chile, pages 8 and 35
JOSUÉ REMACHE (age not given), Ecuador, page 9
PERRY CHEN WEIDA, Age 5, Singapore, page 10
PABLO CABELLO, Age 7, Chile, pages 11 and 23
HØGSET (full name not given), Age 14, Norway, page 13*
HO PEI RONG, Age 12, Singapore, page 14
ANNE-MARIE COUTO, Age 7, China, page 15
ANYA BISCHENKO, Age 11, Russia, page 17
DENNIS TAMBLEY, Age 7, Chile, page 18
NERY BRIONES PADILLA, Age 11, Brazil, page 19
NICK VIDAL (age not given), Peru, page 20
CONAR MCHUGH, Age 8, Ireland, page 21
NATHALY MARIANELA JÁCOME RODRÍGUEZ (age not given), Ecuador, page 22
TASHA JAKIMOFF, Age 11, Australia, page 24
LO MIN MING, Age 10, Singapore, page 25

LAURA CAPELLO, Age 9, Italy, page 26*
JEAN TAN, Age 12, Singapore, page 27
LAURA AHUMADA NATALIA GIACONI (age not given), Chile, page 28
DAISY ESPINOZA (age not given), Ecuador, page 29
CHERYL LOH WAI MAY, Age 10, Malaysia, page 30
ROBERT WILLIAM KRETSCHMER, Age 12, Australia, page 31
PETA CASSIDY, Age 12, Australia, page 32
JEREMY XIE WENQIAN, Age 8, Singapore, page 33
YURIKO TANAKA, Age 5, Japan, page 34
SOFIA ABRANTES, Age 7, Portugal, page 36
SINEAD BROWNE, Age 7, Ireland, page 37
OW CHIANN HUEY, Age 8, Singapore, page 38
KATHERINE JANICE GORDON, Age 12, Australia, page 39
KATHRYN STEWART, Age 6, Australia, page 40
GEMMA KELLY, Age 7, Ireland, page 41
GOH JIAN TONG, Age 11, Singapore, page 42
ALICIA MITCHELL, Age 12, Australia, page 43
MAYRA GARRA GALMA (age not given) Ecuador, page 44

*Used by permission of the International Museum of Children's Art, Oslo, Norway

## THIS BOOK WOULD NOT HAVE BEEN POSSIBLE WITHOUT THE EFFORTS OF THE FOLLOWING ORGANIZATIONS:

BRAHMA KUMARIS WORLD SPIRITUAL UNIVERSITY, editors and publishers of *Visions of a Better World*, a United Nations Peace Messenger publication.

THE WORLD ASSOCIATION OF GIRL GUIDES AND GIRL SCOUTS (WAGGGS), which has member organizations in 129 countries, working to foster international peace by training girls and young women in leadership qualities. WAGGGS' programs are based on spiritual values, informal education, and community service.